Finance Transformed: AI and Blockchain in Action

Empowering Financial Leaders for the Digital Age

Published: November 2024

Author: SHALIN PRAKASH GUPTA

Disclaimer

This book is intended to provide general information and insights into AI and blockchain technologies in finance. While every effort has been made to ensure the accuracy and reliability of the information, the author and publisher assume no responsibility for errors, omissions, or contrary interpretations of the subject matter. The reader is advised to consult with a professional for specific advice and assistance.

This publication is sold with the understanding that neither the author nor the publisher is engaged in rendering legal, financial, or other professional services. Any reliance placed on the contents of this book is strictly at the reader's own risk.

All trademarks mentioned in this book are the property of their respective owners and are used here for identification purposes only. The author and publisher do not claim any ownership of third-party trademarks.

Preface

In recent years, technology has rapidly transformed almost every industry, and finance is no exception. From Artificial Intelligence (AI) to blockchain, emerging technologies are creating a new era of possibilities for finance professionals, students, and tech enthusiasts alike. I wrote this book to help readers explore the power of these transformative tools, understand how they work, and recognize their potential to reshape the finance landscape.

Working with various AI tools like ChatGPT, I have seen firsthand how technology can simplify complex tasks, spark creativity, and generate insights. Through countless hours of experimenting with AI to generate images, videos, and written content, I have gained a deep appreciation for the capabilities—and the challenges—these technologies bring. It's clear that AI and blockchain aren't just trends; they are the building blocks of the future.

This book is designed for anyone looking to gain foundational knowledge about AI and blockchain in finance, whether you're a finance professional wanting to stay current, a student exploring future career options, or a tech enthusiast interested in the intersection of technology and finance. With a conversational and approachable style, I aim to break down complex concepts into easily digestible insights that both beginners and seasoned professionals will find valuable.

As you journey through the chapters, you'll find practical examples, real-world applications, and an honest look at the challenges these technologies present. My hope is that this book will inspire you to explore AI and blockchain further, equipping you with the knowledge and confidence to engage with these exciting fields in meaningful ways.

Thank you for joining me in exploring the future of finance. Let's dive into the incredible world of AI and blockchain and discover together what's next for finance!

TABLE OF CONTENTS

Chapter 1: Introduction to Digital Transformation in Finance

Chapter 2: Foundations of AI in Finance

Chapter 3: Blockchain Basics and Its Potential in Finance

Chapter 4: AI-Powered Processes in Finance

Chapter 5: Blockchain Applications in Finance

Chapter 6: Enhancing Compliance and Security with AI and Blockchain

Chapter 7: Skillsets for Future Finance Professionals

Chapter 8: Ethical, Regulatory, and Implementation Challenges

Chapter 9: Future Trends in AI and Blockchain in Finance

Chapter 10: Conclusion and Practical Takeaways

CHAPTER 1

Introduction to Digital Transformation in Finance

The Shift Toward Digital Finance

The financial world is undergoing a seismic shift, driven by advancements in technology that are reshaping how financial operations are conducted, recorded, and analyzed. Traditional methods in finance—once reliant on manual data entry, paper trails, and periodic audits—are being replaced by automated processes, real-time monitoring, and data-driven decision-making. At the core of this transformation are two revolutionary technologies: **Artificial Intelligence (AI)** and **Blockchain**.

Understanding Digital Transformation

Digital transformation refers to the integration of digital technology into all areas of a business, fundamentally changing how companies operate and deliver value to customers. In finance, digital transformation enables organizations to not only improve efficiency and accuracy but also enhance security and transparency.

Key Drivers of Digital Transformation in Finance:

1. **Increasing Data Volumes**: Financial organizations handle massive volumes of data every day. Digital tools, particularly AI, help process and analyze this data at unprecedented speeds.

2. **Demand for Real-Time Insights**: In today's fast-paced market, decisions must be data-driven and made quickly. Automation and AI provide the tools to perform real-time analysis.
3. **The Need for Enhanced Security**: With the increasing risks of cyber threats, financial institutions require solutions like blockchain for secure, tamper-proof data storage.
4. **Customer Expectations for Transparency**: Modern customers demand transparency and trust, which blockchain's immutable ledger and AI's predictive capabilities can support.

Why AI and Blockchain Are Crucial to Finance

AI and blockchain are not just buzzwords; they represent essential components in the future of finance. As we navigate this transformation, both technologies provide unique solutions that address specific challenges within the industry. AI, for instance, improves efficiency by automating repetitive tasks and delivering advanced analytics, while blockchain brings a level of security and transparency that's particularly valuable for audit and compliance.

Artificial Intelligence (AI):

AI allows for more accurate predictions, enhanced data analysis, and automated processes. By integrating AI into finance, organizations can cut down on human error, accelerate transaction times, and improve customer service.

Blockchain:

Blockchain creates a decentralized and immutable ledger that enhances transparency and security in financial transactions. Every transaction is time-stamped, encrypted, and recorded across a distributed network, making data tamper-proof and reducing the risk of fraud.

Together, AI and blockchain pave the way for a finance sector that is faster, safer, and more innovative than ever before.

How Digital Transformation Redefines Finance

Digital transformation in finance goes beyond just adopting new tools. It requires a shift in mindset and strategy. The finance industry is evolving from a transactional, record-keeping role into a strategic powerhouse that influences business decisions. Thanks to digital transformation, finance professionals now have access to tools that empower them to:

- **Predict Market Trends**: AI models analyze historical data and current trends to forecast future outcomes, giving financial leaders insights that aid in proactive decision-making.

- **Automate Repetitive Tasks**: Tools like Robotic Process Automation (RPA) reduce the time finance teams spend on tasks like invoicing, reconciliation, and reporting.

- **Enhance Security and Trust**: Blockchain's decentralized, tamper-proof ledgers eliminate intermediaries, ensuring that transactions are secure and transparent.

- **Offer Customized Financial Services**: AI can analyze customer behavior to offer tailored recommendations, improving client relationships and satisfaction.

The Changing Role of Finance Professionals

As digital transformation reshapes finance, the role of finance professionals is evolving. Tasks that once required hours of manual work can now be done in minutes by AI or automated systems. This shift allows finance professionals to focus on strategic, high-impact activities, such as financial planning, decision-making, and risk management.

Finance professionals are no longer just record keepers; they are becoming data-driven decision-makers. By leveraging AI for data analysis and blockchain for secure data management, they can provide insights that drive business growth. This evolution requires new skill sets, including data literacy, analytical skills, and an understanding of emerging technologies.

Chapter Summary

Digital transformation in finance, driven by AI and blockchain, is more than a technological upgrade; it's a strategic shift that impacts every aspect of financial operations. Finance teams now have the tools to make real-time decisions, ensure the security of their data, and build trust with customers. As we move through this book, we'll explore the specific ways AI and blockchain are being applied across different finance functions, redefining what's possible in the industry.

CHAPTER 2

Foundations of AI in Finance

What is Artificial Intelligence (AI)?

Artificial Intelligence (AI) refers to the ability of machines to perform tasks that typically require human intelligence. This includes problem-solving, decision-making, and even understanding language. In finance, AI enables systems to analyze data, make predictions, and automate tasks, thus helping professionals focus on strategic decisions rather than routine work.

AI in finance can be divided into two main areas:

1. **Machine Learning (ML)**: A subset of AI where algorithms learn from data to make predictions or decisions. For example, in finance, ML can predict market trends, assess credit risk, and detect fraud.

2. **Robotic Process Automation (RPA)**: RPA uses software robots to automate repetitive tasks, such as invoice processing, data entry, and account reconciliation. It's not as intelligent as ML but greatly improves efficiency.

How AI is Transforming Financial Processes

In the financial industry, AI is improving accuracy, reducing costs, and speeding up operations. Here are some key areas where AI is making a significant impact:

1. **Enhanced Data Processing and Real-Time Analytics**
    - Traditional financial analysis relied on historical data and human interpretation. AI, particularly ML, allows companies to process vast amounts of real-time data to identify trends and make informed predictions.
    - Tools like **IBM Planning Analytics** use AI to scan large datasets, providing real-time insights into financial metrics, KPIs, and market trends.

2. **Automating Routine Tasks**
    - Tasks such as payroll, invoice processing, and bank reconciliation are time-consuming and prone to errors. RPA tools like **UiPath** and **Automation Anywhere** automate these processes, freeing finance professionals for higher-value activities.
    - For instance, an RPA system can process an invoice in minutes, apply tax rules automatically, and route it for approval, all without human intervention.

3. **AI in Financial Forecasting**
    - Forecasting is essential in finance but often involves labor-intensive manual analysis. AI-driven forecasting tools like **Anaplan** and **Workday Adaptive Planning** generate highly accurate predictions based on historical and external data.
    - By analyzing variables such as market conditions, economic trends, and consumer behavior, AI provides more reliable forecasts, helping businesses plan their budgets, allocate resources, and mitigate risks.

4. **AI in Fraud Detection and Risk Management**
    - Fraud detection used to rely on rule-based systems, which struggled to keep up with sophisticated fraud

schemes. Machine learning models now analyze transaction data in real-time, identifying patterns and anomalies that signal potential fraud.

- Tools like **FICO Falcon Fraud Manager** and **SAS Fraud Management** use machine learning to monitor transactions for irregularities, allowing companies to detect fraud as it happens, rather than after the fact.

5. AI-Driven Client Personalization

- In wealth management, AI can assess a client's financial behaviors and risk tolerance to recommend personalized investment strategies. For example, platforms like **Personetics** analyze transaction data to provide tailored financial advice and notifications.

Real-World Examples of AI in Finance

AI isn't just a concept—it's being applied by companies worldwide to transform finance. Here are some notable examples:

- **JP Morgan's COiN**: COiN (Contract Intelligence) is an AI-powered solution that reviews and interprets legal documents. By using machine learning, it can analyze thousands of loan agreements in seconds, identifying key terms and clauses and ensuring compliance.

- **BlackRock's Aladdin**: BlackRock uses an AI-driven platform called Aladdin to manage its investments. Aladdin performs risk assessments, predicts market movements, and suggests investment strategies based on historical data.

- **American Express**: American Express uses machine learning algorithms to detect fraud in real time. These algorithms analyze thousands of transactions per second, flagging suspicious activity and preventing potential fraud.

Key Benefits of AI in Finance

AI in finance brings many benefits, but some stand out for their impact on business operations:

1. **Efficiency and Cost Reduction**: By automating routine tasks and streamlining processes, AI reduces operational costs and improves productivity.
2. **Enhanced Accuracy**: Machine learning models analyze data with high precision, reducing errors and ensuring consistency in reporting and forecasting.
3. **Proactive Risk Management**: AI tools detect potential risks early, allowing finance teams to take preventive action and avoid costly losses.
4. **Improved Customer Experience**: Personalized recommendations and faster response times help organizations provide better service, improving client satisfaction.

Challenges and Considerations in Implementing AI

Despite its benefits, AI in finance also comes with challenges. Implementing AI requires careful planning, a skilled workforce, and robust data infrastructure. Some of the primary challenges include:

1. **Data Privacy and Security**: AI relies on vast amounts of data, some of which is sensitive. Finance companies must ensure data security and comply with regulations, like GDPR, to protect customer information.
2. **Bias in AI Algorithms**: AI systems are only as good as the data they're trained on. If the data is biased, the AI's predictions and decisions will also be biased, which can lead to ethical and regulatory issues.

3. **High Costs of Implementation**: Building and maintaining AI systems can be costly, especially for small to mid-sized finance firms.

4. **Change Management**: Adopting AI may require changes in company culture and processes. Finance teams need to adapt to new workflows and learn how to leverage AI insights effectively.

Chapter Summary

AI is revolutionizing finance by providing tools that enhance accuracy, speed up processes, and improve decision-making. From fraud detection to financial forecasting, AI offers a range of applications that empower finance professionals to focus on strategic tasks. However, implementing AI comes with challenges, particularly around data security, algorithmic bias, and organizational change. As we continue, we'll explore the unique role of blockchain in finance and how it complements AI to create a secure, transparent financial ecosystem.

CHAPTER 3

Blockchain Basics and Its Potential in Finance

Understanding Blockchain Technology

Blockchain is a distributed ledger technology that enables secure, transparent, and tamper-proof record-keeping. Unlike traditional databases, where data is stored in a centralized location, blockchain stores information across a network of computers, called nodes. Every transaction is encrypted, timestamped, and linked to the previous transaction, creating a chain of blocks that cannot be altered without the consensus of the entire network.

Key Characteristics of Blockchain:

1. **Decentralization**: Unlike centralized systems, blockchain is a decentralized network. Transactions are recorded across a distributed network, eliminating the need for a central authority or intermediary.

2. **Immutability**: Once data is recorded on the blockchain, it cannot be altered or deleted. This ensures a permanent, tamper-proof record, making blockchain ideal for audit trails and fraud prevention.

3. **Transparency**: Blockchain provides a transparent ledger that all authorized users can access. This transparency builds trust, as all parties have access to the same version of the truth.

4. **Security**: Blockchain transactions are encrypted, and every block is linked to the previous one. This makes it nearly impossible to alter or hack the data, providing an extra layer of security.

How Blockchain is Transforming Finance

Blockchain technology is reshaping finance by enhancing security, transparency, and efficiency. Here's a look at some of the primary ways blockchain is transforming the financial sector:

1. Blockchain for Enhanced Transparency and Trust

Blockchain's transparency and immutability create a secure environment for financial transactions. Every transaction is recorded in real-time and accessible to all participants in the network. This "single source of truth" reduces the need for intermediaries to verify transactions, builds trust among stakeholders, and simplifies reconciliation.

- **Example**: In supply chain finance, companies use blockchain to track assets, ensuring every transaction is visible to both suppliers and buyers. IBM's Blockchain for Trade Finance allows companies to trace the movement of goods, helping reduce fraud and build trust among trading partners.

2. Real-Time Auditing with Blockchain

Auditing has traditionally been a time-consuming process involving manual data checks and reconciliations. Blockchain enables real-time auditing by providing continuous access to verified transaction data. Auditors can access financial records instantly and verify transactions as they occur, reducing the time and cost associated with traditional audits.

- **Example**: **EY's Blockchain Analyzer** allows auditors to review and verify blockchain transactions in real-time, enabling more efficient and accurate audits. This tool allows companies to meet regulatory requirements without the usual delays and paperwork.

3. Fraud Prevention through Immutable Records

Blockchain's immutable ledger prevents tampering, making it an effective tool for fraud prevention. Because every transaction is securely recorded and cannot be altered, blockchain creates a verifiable audit trail that deters fraudulent activities.

- **Example**: **J.P. Morgan's Quorum** blockchain platform enhances fraud detection by providing a secure, tamper-proof ledger for financial transactions. By making transaction data transparent and immutable, Quorum reduces the risk of fraud and enhances regulatory compliance.

4. Streamlining Compliance and Regulatory Reporting

Financial institutions face rigorous compliance requirements and must provide accurate records to regulators. Blockchain simplifies compliance by creating an immutable, time-stamped record of every transaction, which can be easily accessed for audits or regulatory reviews. This streamlining not only saves time but also reduces the risk of errors or non-compliance.

- **Example**: **HSBC** uses blockchain to streamline its trade finance processes, allowing it to create transparent, auditable records of all transactions, simplifying the compliance process and reducing fraud.

5. Smart Contracts for Automation in Finance

Smart contracts are self-executing contracts where the terms of the agreement are written directly into code. When specific conditions are met, the contract automatically executes actions, such as transferring funds or releasing goods. Smart contracts eliminate the need for intermediaries, reduce transaction costs, and enable faster, more reliable transactions.

- **Example**: **Santander Bank** uses smart contracts on the blockchain to simplify international payments. These smart contracts automatically execute cross-border payments, reducing the time and cost associated with traditional banking processes.

Real-World Applications of Blockchain in Finance

Blockchain technology is already being adopted by financial institutions and companies worldwide. Here are some prominent examples:

- **Mastercard's Blockchain-Based Payments**: Mastercard has implemented blockchain technology to secure its payment processes, allowing for faster, traceable, and more secure transactions.
- **De Beers' Diamond Tracking**: De Beers, the diamond company, uses blockchain to track diamonds from the mine to the market, ensuring authenticity and ethical sourcing. This transparency helps combat counterfeit goods and builds consumer trust.
- **PwC's Blockchain Validation Service**: PwC provides a blockchain validation service that helps organizations verify their blockchain-based records. This service enhances transparency and ensures that financial records meet regulatory standards.

Key Benefits of Blockchain in Finance

Blockchain offers multiple benefits that address critical needs in the financial sector:

1. **Security and Fraud Prevention**: Blockchain's cryptographic security and immutability make it highly resistant to fraud, ensuring the integrity of financial records.

2. **Transparency and Trust**: All parties in a blockchain network share the same version of the ledger, building trust and reducing disputes over discrepancies.

3. **Cost Efficiency**: By eliminating intermediaries and reducing the need for manual verification, blockchain lowers transaction costs and speeds up processes.

4. **Regulatory Compliance**: Blockchain's timestamped, immutable records make it easy for organizations to meet compliance requirements and provide transparent reports to regulators.

Challenges in Implementing Blockchain in Finance

Despite its potential, blockchain also faces some challenges that financial institutions must consider:

1. **Scalability**: As the number of transactions grows, the blockchain can become slower and more resource-intensive. This is particularly challenging for large financial institutions.

2. **Regulatory Uncertainty**: The regulatory landscape for blockchain is still evolving, and inconsistent regulations can hinder widespread adoption.

3. **Integration with Legacy Systems**: Many financial institutions rely on legacy systems, and integrating blockchain with these systems can be complex and costly.

4. **Security and Privacy**: While blockchain is secure, its transparency can raise privacy concerns, especially for institutions handling sensitive financial data.

Chapter Summary

Blockchain technology is fundamentally changing finance by providing secure, transparent, and tamper-proof solutions for record-keeping, compliance, and fraud prevention. Its decentralized nature eliminates the need for intermediaries, while smart contracts enable automation and reduce transaction costs. However, implementing blockchain also presents challenges, particularly in scalability, regulation, and integration. Together with AI, blockchain is creating a finance industry that is more efficient, secure, and trustworthy.

CHAPTER 4

AI-Powered Processes in Finance

Revolutionizing Finance Through AI Applications

AI's impact on finance goes beyond basic automation. By integrating machine learning algorithms, predictive analytics, and natural language processing, AI is transforming how finance professionals analyze data, detect fraud, make predictions, and provide personalized services. Here are the key areas where AI is creating significant change in finance.

1. Data Processing and Real-Time Auditing

Traditional auditing involves labor-intensive processes that often rely on historical data. AI-powered systems can now process vast datasets in real time, allowing for continuous auditing. This enables finance teams to identify errors, flag potential fraud, and ensure compliance more efficiently.

- **Example**: AI-driven tools like **MindBridge Ai Auditor** analyze financial transactions to identify anomalies and unusual patterns that might indicate fraud. By processing transactions in real time, these tools allow auditors to focus on riskier areas while reducing the time spent on manual reviews.

2. Predictive Analytics and Financial Forecasting

Financial forecasting has always been essential to business strategy, but traditional forecasting models rely heavily on historical data and manual assumptions. AI, however, brings a new level of precision to forecasting by analyzing not only past data but also external factors like market conditions and customer behaviors.

- **Example**: **IBM's Watson Analytics** uses predictive analytics to identify trends and patterns in financial data, enabling companies to forecast revenue, expenses, and cash flows with higher accuracy. This allows finance leaders to make informed decisions about resource allocation, risk management, and investment.

3. Automating Routine Financial Tasks

Many finance professionals spend a significant amount of time on routine tasks such as processing invoices, managing payroll, and reconciling accounts. Robotic Process Automation (RPA), a subset of AI, is well-suited for these repetitive tasks, allowing finance teams to focus on more strategic work.

- **Example**: **UiPath** and **Automation Anywhere** offer RPA tools that automate tasks like invoice processing and payroll management. These tools can read invoices, verify payment details, and even handle exceptions without human intervention.

4. AI for Fraud Detection and Risk Management

Fraud detection in finance has traditionally been rule-based, relying on static rules to flag unusual transactions. AI takes fraud detection to the next level by using machine learning algorithms to analyze transaction data in real-time and identify patterns that human analysts might miss.

- **Example**: **FICO Falcon Fraud Manager** uses machine learning to monitor credit card transactions for irregularities, flagging suspicious activity as it happens. This reduces losses due to fraud and helps protect customer data.

5. Personalization in Financial Services

In wealth management and retail banking, AI is enhancing customer experience by providing personalized financial advice and services. AI can analyze a client's spending patterns, investment preferences, and risk tolerance to recommend tailored solutions that meet their unique financial goals.

- **Example**: **Personetics** is an AI-powered platform that helps banks deliver personalized insights and product recommendations. By analyzing customer behavior and transaction data, Personetics enables financial institutions to provide highly customized advice, improving client relationships and satisfaction.

6. Chatbots and Virtual Assistants for Customer Support

Customer support is a vital part of financial services, and AI chatbots are increasingly used to provide fast, accurate, and 24/7 service to clients. These chatbots handle common customer inquiries, provide financial advice, and even assist with tasks like loan applications or account updates.

- **Example**: **Capital One's Eno** is an AI-driven virtual assistant that helps customers track spending, monitor account activity, and receive real-time updates on transactions. Eno's personalized assistance improves customer engagement and satisfaction by providing instant responses to customer questions.

Real-World Impact of AI-Driven Processes

AI-powered processes in finance are already delivering tangible benefits, such as improved efficiency, reduced operational costs, and enhanced customer satisfaction. By automating routine tasks, finance teams can focus on more complex activities, and by enhancing fraud detection, companies can protect both their assets and reputation.

Here are some additional real-world examples:

- **American Express**: The company uses machine learning models to detect fraudulent transactions. By analyzing millions of transactions in real-time, American Express can flag suspicious activities immediately, protecting both its customers and its bottom line.

- **KPMG Clara**: KPMG has developed an AI-driven audit platform called Clara, which enables continuous monitoring and real-time auditing. Clara scans transactions for anomalies, allowing auditors to focus on high-risk areas and improve the quality of audits.

- **BlackLine**: BlackLine automates financial close processes such as account reconciliations and transaction matching. By integrating AI and RPA, BlackLine reduces the manual effort involved in closing books, making the process faster and more accurate.

Key Benefits of AI in Finance Processes

The benefits of AI in finance processes are profound, reshaping the industry in several ways:

1. **Enhanced Efficiency**: By automating repetitive tasks, AI saves time and reduces operational costs, allowing finance teams to focus on strategic initiatives.

2. **Improved Accuracy**: AI minimizes the risk of human error, ensuring more accurate data processing, reporting, and forecasting.

3. **Real-Time Insights**: AI provides real-time data analysis, enabling proactive decision-making and

risk management.

4. **Better Risk Detection**: Machine learning models can identify potential risks early, allowing companies to take preventive action.

5. **Superior Customer Experience**: Personalized financial advice and instant responses improve customer satisfaction and loyalty.

Challenges in AI-Powered Finance Processes

While AI offers many benefits, it also presents challenges:

1. **Data Quality and Privacy**: AI relies on large datasets, and poor data quality can lead to inaccurate results. Finance companies also need to ensure data privacy and comply with regulations.

2. **Algorithm Bias**: AI algorithms can inherit biases from the data they're trained on, leading to potential ethical and fairness issues in areas like lending or risk assessment.

3. **High Implementation Costs**: Building and maintaining AI-powered systems require significant investment, which may be a barrier for smaller firms.

4. **Skill Requirements**: Finance professionals need data analysis and technical skills to work effectively with AI tools, creating a need for continuous upskilling.

Chapter Summary

AI-powered processes are transforming finance, enabling companies to automate repetitive tasks, improve accuracy, and gain real-time insights. From fraud detection to customer personalization, AI applications are enhancing the quality and efficiency of financial operations. However, implementing AI requires attention to data quality, regulatory compliance, and skilled personnel. As we move forward, we'll explore how blockchain contributes to a secure, transparent financial ecosystem, further complementing AI's capabilities.

CHAPTER 5

Blockchain Applications in Finance

The Unique Role of Blockchain in Finance

Blockchain technology is gaining traction in finance due to its unique ability to create secure, transparent, and tamper-proof records. Financial institutions and companies around the world are increasingly using blockchain to address longstanding challenges like data security, fraud prevention, and compliance. In this chapter, we will explore how blockchain's unique characteristics are being applied to enhance transparency, streamline processes, and improve security across various financial functions.

1. Enhanced Transparency and Trust in Financial Transactions

Blockchain's decentralized ledger system offers unparalleled transparency, creating a shared, single version of the truth accessible to all authorized participants. This transparency eliminates the need for intermediaries, minimizes the chance of discrepancies, and enhances trust between stakeholders.

- **Example**: IBM's Food Trust Network applies blockchain to track the movement of food through supply chains, ensuring each transaction is visible to suppliers, retailers, and consumers. Similarly, in finance, blockchain can help trace the flow of funds, reducing fraud and increasing transparency in transactions between parties.

2. Real-Time Auditing and Continuous Monitoring

Traditional auditing relies on periodic checks and manual reconciliation, making it a slow, resource-intensive process. Blockchain enables real-time auditing, as each transaction is recorded and verified instantly. This continuous monitoring allows auditors and regulators to access accurate, up-to-date data, simplifying the compliance process and improving accuracy.

- **Example**: **PwC's Blockchain Validation Service** supports real-time auditing by enabling companies to verify blockchain transactions for accuracy and compliance. This service helps reduce audit costs and provides regulators with instant access to financial records, eliminating delays in reporting.

3. Fraud Prevention and Security

Financial fraud is a major issue in the industry, and blockchain offers a robust solution to address this challenge. Blockchain's immutable ledger makes it nearly impossible to alter transaction records, creating a verifiable trail that deters fraud and increases accountability. By reducing the risk of tampering, blockchain strengthens security and minimizes fraudulent activities.

- **Example**: **Mastercard's Blockchain-Based Payments** enhances security in payment transactions. By recording each transaction on an immutable ledger, Mastercard minimizes fraud risk, allowing customers and businesses to process payments with greater confidence.

4. Smart Contracts and Process Automation

Smart contracts are self-executing contracts in which the terms of the agreement are written directly into code. These contracts automatically execute specific actions, such as releasing funds or transferring assets, when predetermined conditions are met. Smart contracts eliminate the need for intermediaries, reduce transaction costs, and enable faster, more secure transactions.

- **Example**: **Santander Bank** uses blockchain-based smart contracts to streamline cross-border payments, reducing transaction times and cutting out middlemen. By executing payments instantly when conditions are met, Santander improves efficiency and reduces the costs of traditional international transactions.

5. Streamlining Compliance and Regulatory Reporting

Blockchain's ability to create secure, timestamped records simplifies regulatory reporting and compliance. Each transaction is logged in an immutable ledger that regulators can access in real time, reducing the need for manual data collection and ensuring that companies stay compliant with ease.

- **Example**: **HSBC** leverages blockchain in trade finance to create digital records of international transactions, which simplifies compliance and minimizes the risk of human error. By digitizing the trade finance process, HSBC provides regulators with real-time access to transaction data, streamlining reporting and compliance requirements.

Decentralized Finance (DeFi): The Next Frontier

Decentralized Finance (DeFi) is an emerging trend within blockchain that seeks to create an open, global financial system. DeFi platforms enable users to lend, borrow, trade, and invest without intermediaries, offering a more efficient, accessible, and transparent alternative to traditional financial systems.

How DeFi Works: DeFi platforms are built on public blockchains, allowing anyone with internet access to participate. Through smart contracts, DeFi platforms offer services like loans, insurance, and trading, which are governed by code rather than institutions. This transparency reduces fees, increases access, and democratizes finance.

- **Example**: **Compound** and **AAVE** are popular DeFi platforms that allow users to lend or borrow digital assets directly without a bank. This eliminates the need for traditional financial intermediaries, providing users with faster, more cost-effective access to financial services.

Key Benefits of Blockchain in Finance

1. **Enhanced Security**: Blockchain's cryptographic nature and decentralized architecture make it highly resistant to fraud and cyberattacks, ensuring secure transactions.
2. **Improved Transparency**: Every transaction on the blockchain is visible to authorized parties, creating a transparent and auditable record that builds trust among stakeholders.
3. **Cost Efficiency**: By reducing the need for intermediaries, blockchain lowers transaction fees and speeds up processes, making finance more efficient.
4. **Compliance Simplification**: Blockchain's immutable ledger makes it easy for companies to meet regulatory requirements, as all transaction records are readily available and verifiable.
5. **Increased Accessibility**: With DeFi, blockchain offers access to financial services for individuals who may lack traditional banking options, fostering financial inclusion.

Challenges of Blockchain Implementation in Finance

Despite the benefits, blockchain implementation comes with challenges:

1. **Scalability Issues**: Blockchain networks can experience slow processing times as the number of transactions grows, making it challenging for large financial institutions to adopt the technology on a large scale.
2. **Regulatory Concerns**: The legal and regulatory framework for blockchain is still evolving, and uncertainty can be a barrier to adoption, particularly in highly regulated sectors like finance.
3. **Integration with Legacy Systems**: Many financial institutions rely on legacy systems, and integrating blockchain into these systems can be costly and complex.
4. **Data Privacy**: Blockchain's transparency may conflict with privacy requirements, as transaction data is visible to all participants on the network. Privacy-focused solutions, such as private blockchains, are being developed but remain in the early stages.

Real-World Applications: Leading Financial Institutions Leveraging Blockchain

Many companies and financial institutions are already adopting blockchain to streamline operations and enhance security. Here are a few notable examples:

- **JP Morgan's Quorum**: This enterprise blockchain platform is used for secure, tamper-proof financial transactions. Quorum enables JP Morgan to provide clients with faster, more transparent banking services while reducing operational risks.
- **De Beers and Provenance Tracking**: De Beers uses blockchain to track diamonds from the mine to

the retail market, ensuring ethical sourcing and authenticity. This level of traceability can also be applied to financial transactions, providing a transparent view of asset ownership.

- **Deloitte's Blockchain Assurance**: Deloitte offers blockchain-based assurance tools to help organizations meet regulatory standards and streamline audits. By providing real-time access to verified financial data, Deloitte's platform helps auditors focus on high-risk areas and improve audit accuracy.

Chapter Summary

Blockchain is revolutionizing finance by offering secure, transparent, and tamper-proof solutions for a range of applications, including auditing, fraud prevention, compliance, and process automation. Decentralized Finance (DeFi) represents an exciting extension of blockchain, enabling financial transactions without traditional intermediaries. However, challenges such as scalability, regulatory uncertainty, and integration with legacy systems remain. As we move forward, blockchain's role in finance will likely grow, helping create a more efficient, secure, and accessible financial ecosystem.

CHAPTER 6

Enhancing Compliance and Security with AI and Blockchain

The Need for Compliance and Security in Finance

In finance, compliance and security are paramount. Financial institutions must adhere to strict regulations to protect consumer data, prevent fraud, and maintain trust. However, as financial data becomes increasingly digital, the risk of cyber threats and data breaches rises. AI and blockchain technologies offer innovative solutions that enhance compliance and security, making it easier for organizations to safeguard data and meet regulatory requirements.

How AI and Blockchain Address Compliance Challenges

AI and **blockchain** provide unique benefits in addressing compliance and security concerns:

1. **AI for Regulatory Compliance**: AI-driven solutions help monitor transactions, analyze risks, and ensure compliance with ever-evolving regulations. Through machine learning algorithms, AI can analyze vast amounts of data to detect patterns and anomalies, allowing finance teams to proactively address compliance issues.

2. **Blockchain for Data Integrity**: Blockchain's immutable ledger ensures that once data is recorded,

it cannot be altered, making it ideal for compliance and record-keeping. This tamper-proof nature of blockchain helps institutions maintain accurate, transparent records, which auditors and regulators can access in real time.

Key Applications of AI and Blockchain in Compliance and Security

1. Automated Compliance Monitoring with AI

Traditionally, compliance monitoring is a manual and time-consuming task that requires teams to review large datasets to identify any deviations from regulatory standards. AI simplifies this process by continuously analyzing transaction data for any signs of non-compliance.

- **Example**: **Ayasdi AML** is an AI-powered anti-money laundering solution that uses machine learning to detect patterns in financial transactions. It identifies suspicious activities, such as unusual transaction volumes or fund transfers, helping banks meet anti-money laundering (AML) requirements more efficiently.

2. Fraud Detection and Risk Management with AI

AI-powered fraud detection systems use machine learning to analyze transaction data in real time, identifying anomalies that may indicate fraudulent activity. This proactive approach allows organizations to prevent fraud before it escalates.

- **Example**: **Darktrace** uses AI to monitor network traffic and detect unusual behavior that may indicate cyber threats or insider fraud. Darktrace's system continuously learns from new data, allowing it to identify even the most sophisticated cyber threats, protecting both customer data and financial assets.

3. Blockchain for Secure Data Storage and Integrity

Blockchain's decentralized architecture ensures that financial data is stored securely across multiple nodes, reducing the risk of data tampering and breaches. Every transaction recorded on the blockchain is time-stamped and verified, creating a permanent record that cannot be altered.

- **Example**: **HSBC** uses blockchain in trade finance to create secure records of international transactions. By leveraging blockchain's tamper-proof features, HSBC can provide regulators with instant access to transaction data, enhancing both security and compliance.

4. Smart Contracts for Compliance Automation

Smart contracts automate compliance processes by embedding regulatory rules directly into the contract code. Once specific conditions are met, the smart contract automatically executes the necessary actions, such as verifying funds or completing a transaction.

- **Example**: **Aetna and IBM** use blockchain-powered smart contracts in healthcare to automate data-sharing and compliance checks. In finance, similar smart contracts could automate compliance with regulations such as Know Your Customer (KYC) or AML, reducing the administrative burden on financial institutions.

5. Identity Verification and KYC Compliance

Know Your Customer (KYC) regulations require financial institutions to verify the identity of their clients to prevent fraud and money laundering. Blockchain can streamline KYC by creating a secure, digital identity for each customer. Once verified, these digital identities can be securely shared across institutions, reducing the need for repetitive checks.

- **Example**: **Civic** is a blockchain-based identity verification platform that allows users to create a digital identity on the blockchain. Financial institutions can use Civic's platform to securely verify customer identities and streamline the KYC process, making it faster and more secure.

Benefits of AI and Blockchain for Compliance and Security

1. **Improved Accuracy and Efficiency**: AI reduces manual effort in compliance by automating data analysis and anomaly detection, ensuring more accurate results with less human intervention.

2. **Enhanced Fraud Prevention**: AI-driven systems identify fraudulent activity as it happens, allowing institutions to act immediately. Blockchain's immutable ledger provides an extra layer of fraud prevention by securing transaction records.

3. **Transparency and Accountability**: Blockchain provides a transparent record of every transaction, which can be accessed by regulators in real-time. This transparency fosters accountability and simplifies audits.

4. **Cost Savings**: Automating compliance processes reduces costs associated with manual monitoring, data verification, and fraud prevention.

5. **Simplified Reporting**: Blockchain's timestamped records simplify regulatory reporting, as transaction data is readily accessible and easily verified by regulators.

Challenges in AI and Blockchain Compliance and Security

Despite their benefits, AI and blockchain also present challenges in the context of compliance and security:

1. **Data Privacy and Confidentiality**: Blockchain's transparency can conflict with data privacy regulations like GDPR, which require data to be erasable upon request. Private blockchains or permissioned access can help address this issue, but these solutions are still evolving.

2. **Complexity of AI Models**: Machine learning models can be complex and may produce results that are difficult for regulators and stakeholders to interpret. This "black-box" issue can complicate compliance with transparency requirements.

3. **Integration with Legacy Systems**: Many financial institutions still rely on legacy systems, which can be challenging to integrate with newer AI and blockchain technologies.

4. **High Implementation Costs**: Implementing AI and blockchain requires significant investment in technology, data management, and skilled personnel, which can be a barrier for smaller firms.

Future Trends in Compliance and Security with AI and Blockchain

The future of compliance and security in finance will likely see even deeper integration of AI and blockchain as these technologies mature. Some emerging trends include:

- **Privacy-Enhancing Technologies (PETs)**: As data privacy concerns grow, blockchain and AI solutions are incorporating PETs, such as zero-knowledge proofs, to verify compliance without exposing sensitive data.

- **Federated Learning**: Federated learning allows machine learning models to train on decentralized data, making it possible to develop robust AI systems without sharing raw data. This approach could help financial institutions protect privacy while maintaining compliance.

- **Self-Regulating Smart Contracts**: Future smart contracts may include built-in regulatory frameworks that automatically adjust based on updated compliance requirements, reducing the need for manual intervention.

Chapter Summary

AI and blockchain are transforming compliance and security in finance, helping institutions meet regulatory requirements, prevent fraud, and enhance data security. AI's ability to automate compliance monitoring and blockchain's tamper-proof records provide powerful tools for managing risk. While challenges remain, such as data privacy concerns and integration costs, the potential benefits make these technologies essential for the future of secure, compliant financial operations.

CHAPTER 7

Skillsets for Future Finance Professionals

The Evolving Role of Finance Professionals

As AI and blockchain reshape the financial landscape, the skillset required for finance professionals is evolving. Tasks that were once manual and time-consuming, such as data entry, reconciliation, and compliance checks, are now automated. This shift allows finance professionals to focus on high-level, strategic roles that require a deeper understanding of technology, data analysis, and regulatory frameworks.

To thrive in a technology-driven finance sector, professionals need to develop both technical and soft skills. Here's an overview of the key competencies that will be in demand in the future of finance.

Key Skillsets for the Modern Finance Professional

1. Data Literacy and Analytical Skills

As AI and data analytics become central to financial operations, data literacy is essential. Finance professionals must be able to interpret data, understand analytics, and leverage insights for decision-making.

- **Data Interpretation**: Understanding how to read data outputs and spot trends is crucial for data-driven decision-making.

- **Statistical Analysis**: Basic knowledge of statistics is valuable for understanding AI models and performing financial analysis.
- **Tool Familiarity**: Familiarity with data analytics tools like **Tableau**, **Power BI**, and **Excel** enables professionals to visualize data and extract insights.

2. Understanding of AI and Machine Learning

While finance professionals aren't expected to be AI engineers, a foundational understanding of AI concepts, such as machine learning, predictive analytics, and RPA, is important. This knowledge will allow them to work effectively with AI-driven tools, evaluate AI outputs, and understand their potential applications in finance.

- **AI Concepts**: Knowledge of basic AI concepts, such as supervised and unsupervised learning, helps finance professionals understand how AI models function.
- **Practical Application**: Understanding specific AI applications in finance, such as fraud detection or forecasting, enables professionals to leverage these tools in their roles.
- **Collaboration with Data Scientists**: As AI implementation grows, finance professionals will work closely with data scientists, so an understanding of AI terminology and processes will aid communication and collaboration.

3. Blockchain Literacy

Blockchain technology offers transformative potential, particularly in areas like compliance, auditing, and transaction security. A basic understanding of how blockchain works, including concepts like decentralization, smart contracts, and cryptography, will be beneficial for finance professionals.

- **Blockchain Fundamentals**: Familiarity with key concepts, such as how transactions are validated and recorded, helps professionals understand blockchain's value in finance.

- **Smart Contracts**: Understanding the role of smart contracts and their applications in automating agreements is particularly valuable for roles related to compliance and auditing.

- **Regulatory Implications**: Knowledge of the regulatory environment surrounding blockchain is crucial, as blockchain technology can impact areas like data privacy and financial compliance.

4. Cybersecurity Awareness

As finance becomes more digital, the need for cybersecurity is paramount. Finance professionals should have an awareness of cybersecurity best practices, particularly when handling sensitive financial data. This includes understanding data protection laws, encryption techniques, and secure data storage.

- **Data Protection**: Knowing how to protect sensitive data and ensure compliance with regulations like GDPR or CCPA is essential for safeguarding financial information.

- **Cybersecurity Risks**: Understanding common threats, such as phishing and data breaches, helps finance professionals mitigate risks and respond appropriately.

- **Collaboration with IT**: Professionals who work closely with cybersecurity and IT teams can better protect financial data and reduce the risk of breaches.

5. Compliance and Regulatory Knowledge

With the integration of AI and blockchain, finance professionals must stay informed of evolving regulations to ensure compliance. Knowledge of industry standards, such as AML, KYC, and data privacy laws, is crucial for maintaining regulatory compliance in a technology-driven environment.

- **Industry Regulations**: Familiarity with financial regulations, especially those related to digital transactions, is essential for roles focused on compliance and auditing.
- **Ethical and Legal Considerations**: Understanding the ethical implications of AI and blockchain, such as algorithmic bias and data privacy, ensures responsible use of these technologies.
- **Continuous Learning**: Since regulations are constantly evolving, finance professionals must stay updated through courses, webinars, and industry publications.

6. Strategic Thinking and Problem-Solving Skills

As finance becomes more strategic, professionals must possess strong problem-solving abilities and a strategic mindset. They should be able to assess financial data, consider technological solutions, and make decisions that align with business objectives.

- **Analytical Mindset**: Critical thinking and the ability to analyze complex situations are essential for evaluating financial data and identifying trends.
- **Decision-Making**: As automation handles routine tasks, finance professionals will focus on making high-level decisions, such as resource allocation and risk management.
- **Technology Integration**: Understanding how to integrate AI and blockchain into existing financial

processes allows finance teams to leverage these tools effectively for strategic gains.

7. Adaptability and Continuous Learning

Technology is evolving rapidly, and finance professionals must be adaptable and open to learning. This may involve pursuing certifications in AI, data analytics, or blockchain, attending industry seminars, or completing online courses to stay updated on the latest advancements.

- **Certifications and Training**: Courses in data analytics, machine learning, and blockchain can enhance skills and increase job market competitiveness.

- **Industry Updates**: Staying informed of technological advancements through finance publications, webinars, and professional networks is essential for continuous growth.

- **Learning Agility**: Adaptability is key in a field that's constantly evolving. Finance professionals who embrace change and actively seek to expand their skillsets will thrive in a technology-driven environment.

Real-World Examples of Skills in Action

Many finance organizations are already emphasizing these skillsets as they adopt AI and blockchain. Here are some examples:

- **Deloitte's Analytics Academy**: Deloitte offers training programs in data analytics, AI, and blockchain to help its finance teams develop technical and analytical skills.

- **HSBC's Cybersecurity Training**: HSBC prioritizes cybersecurity awareness training for its finance teams, ensuring they understand best practices in data protection and regulatory compliance.

- **EY's Blockchain Certification Program**: EY provides a blockchain certification program that helps finance professionals understand how to implement blockchain technology in areas like auditing and compliance.

Building Your Skillset: Resources and Tools

1. **Online Learning Platforms**: Websites like **Coursera**, **edX**, and **LinkedIn Learning** offer courses in AI, blockchain, data analytics, and cybersecurity tailored to finance professionals.

2. **Certifications**: Industry-recognized certifications, such as Certified Information Systems Auditor (CISA), Certified Financial Analyst (CFA), and Certified Blockchain Expert (CBE), can provide specialized knowledge in these areas.

3. **Networking**: Joining professional groups, attending conferences, and connecting with technology experts on LinkedIn are excellent ways to stay informed and learn from peers.

4. **Professional Journals and Publications**: Subscribing to finance and technology journals, such as **Harvard Business Review** or **MIT Technology Review**, provides regular updates on industry trends and technological advancements.

Chapter Summary

The finance professional of the future will need a mix of technical and strategic skills, including data literacy, AI and blockchain knowledge, cybersecurity awareness, and a solid understanding of compliance regulations. As finance becomes increasingly digital, these skills will enable professionals to make data-driven decisions, leverage emerging technologies, and address new challenges in a complex regulatory environment. Continuous learning and adaptability are essential as technology advances, shaping a finance sector that's both innovative and secure.

CHAPTER 8

Ethical, Regulatory, and Implementation Challenges

The Intersection of Ethics, Regulation, and Technology

The adoption of AI and blockchain in finance brings tremendous benefits, but it also raises important ethical, regulatory, and implementation challenges. As these technologies become more integrated into financial operations, finance professionals and regulators must address potential risks, including data privacy issues, algorithmic bias, and regulatory compliance. In this chapter, we explore these challenges and discuss ways to address them.

1. Ethical Challenges

Algorithmic Bias and Fairness

AI algorithms are only as unbiased as the data on which they are trained. If the training data contains biases, the AI model may make decisions that unfairly discriminate against certain individuals or groups. In finance, this can be particularly problematic in areas like lending, credit scoring, and fraud detection, where biased algorithms may impact customers' access to services or financial opportunities.

- **Example**: A machine learning model used for credit scoring might inadvertently discriminate against applicants from certain demographics if the training data is biased. Such bias could lead to unfair denial of loans or credit services, violating principles of fairness and equality.

Solution: To address algorithmic bias, finance organizations can implement regular audits of AI models and incorporate fairness checks into their development process. Diverse and representative data sets, combined with transparent model training processes, help reduce the risk of bias.

Transparency and Explainability

AI models, especially complex machine learning models, can act as "black boxes," making decisions without providing clear explanations. This lack of transparency can create challenges in regulatory compliance and customer trust, as clients and regulators may demand clarity on how certain decisions were made.

- **Example**: If an AI model flags a transaction as fraudulent, customers and regulators may require an explanation of the specific factors that led to this decision. Without explainability, the decision could be questioned, impacting trust.

Solution: Finance companies can use explainable AI (XAI) models that provide insights into how decisions are made. Additionally, organizations can maintain documentation of AI decision-making processes, allowing for greater transparency and accountability.

Privacy and Data Ownership

With blockchain and AI heavily reliant on data, privacy is a major concern. Regulations such as the General Data Protection Regulation (GDPR) in the EU mandate that individuals have the right to access, modify, or delete their personal data. Blockchain's immutability can conflict with these requirements, raising concerns about data ownership and control.

- **Example**: On a blockchain, once personal data is recorded, it becomes difficult to delete. This may violate privacy laws that allow individuals to request the deletion of their data.

Solution: Organizations can address privacy concerns by using private or permissioned blockchains, which allow data to be controlled and accessed by authorized users only. Techniques like zero-knowledge proofs and encryption can also help protect sensitive data while maintaining blockchain's security benefits.

2. Regulatory Challenges

Lack of Standardized Regulations

The regulatory landscape for AI and blockchain is still evolving, with different jurisdictions implementing varied laws and guidelines. This lack of standardization creates uncertainty for global financial institutions, as compliance requirements may vary across countries and regions.

- **Example**: In the United States, different states have different regulations on cryptocurrency and blockchain, creating complexity for companies operating across state lines. Similarly, AI regulations vary globally, with some countries adopting stricter policies than others.

Solution: Finance organizations can establish cross-functional compliance teams to stay informed of changing regulations across jurisdictions. Collaborating with regulatory bodies and joining industry groups can also help companies stay updated on new standards and best practices.

Compliance with Data Privacy Laws

Data privacy regulations, like GDPR and the California Consumer Privacy Act (CCPA), require that companies handle personal data responsibly, ensuring customer consent and data protection. These laws create challenges for AI and blockchain implementations, as these technologies often involve extensive data collection and processing.

- **Example**: An AI model that analyzes customer spending patterns to provide personalized financial advice must comply with data privacy regulations, ensuring that customers consent to the use of their data.

Solution: Organizations should implement data governance frameworks to manage customer data responsibly. Obtaining explicit consent, minimizing data collection to what is necessary, and using anonymization techniques are essential steps for maintaining compliance.

AML and KYC Compliance

Anti-money laundering (AML) and Know Your Customer (KYC) regulations require financial institutions to verify the identities of clients and monitor transactions for suspicious activities. Blockchain and AI can support compliance, but they also introduce new regulatory considerations, as regulators may require access to transaction data on the blockchain.

- **Example**: An AI system that monitors transactions for potential money laundering activities must ensure that its algorithms comply with AML standards and that blockchain data can be accessed by regulators when necessary.

Solution: Organizations can use permissioned blockchains to control data access and ensure that KYC information is securely stored. Additionally, AI systems can be programmed to monitor compliance requirements, generating alerts for potentially non-compliant transactions.

3. Implementation Challenges

Integration with Legacy Systems

Many financial institutions rely on legacy systems that may not be compatible with advanced AI and blockchain solutions. Integrating these new technologies into existing infrastructures can be complex and costly, often requiring significant technical expertise and investment.

- **Example**: A bank that wants to implement blockchain for transaction tracking may face challenges if its existing systems aren't designed to interact with a decentralized ledger.

Solution: Financial organizations can take a phased approach to implementation, starting with small-scale pilot projects. Working with third-party vendors and consultants can also help organizations overcome integration challenges and develop tailored solutions that work alongside legacy systems.

High Costs of Implementation

The cost of implementing AI and blockchain is high, particularly for smaller financial institutions that may lack the resources of larger firms. Costs include investments in technology, data infrastructure, training, and ongoing maintenance.

- **Example**: A mid-sized bank may struggle to adopt AI for fraud detection due to the costs of developing and maintaining the system, including data storage, model training, and staff training.

Solution: To manage costs, organizations can consider using open-source tools or partnering with technology providers who offer AI and blockchain solutions as a service. Additionally, training existing staff on AI and blockchain can reduce reliance on expensive external consultants.

Skill Gaps and Workforce Training

AI and blockchain require specialized skills in areas like data science, programming, and cybersecurity. Many finance teams lack these skills, and finding qualified professionals can be challenging.

- **Example**: A finance firm implementing AI for data analysis may struggle to find staff with the necessary knowledge of machine learning algorithms and data processing.

Solution: Finance organizations can invest in training programs to upskill existing employees and close the skills gap. Offering certifications in AI, blockchain, and data analytics can also help attract and retain talent with specialized skills.

Future Directions: Navigating Ethical, Regulatory, and Implementation Challenges

To fully harness the potential of AI and blockchain, finance organizations must address these challenges proactively. As the industry matures, we can expect more standardized regulations, increased access to training, and the development of privacy-enhancing technologies. Ethical AI guidelines, stronger governance frameworks, and collaborative efforts with regulators will be essential in creating a responsible, secure, and transparent financial ecosystem.

Chapter Summary

AI and blockchain bring significant opportunities to the financial sector, but they also introduce ethical, regulatory, and implementation challenges. From algorithmic bias to data privacy concerns, these technologies require careful planning and oversight to ensure responsible use. By investing in compliance, adopting transparent practices, and collaborating with regulatory bodies, finance professionals can navigate these challenges and create a trustworthy, ethical framework for digital finance.

CHAPTER 9

Future Trends in AI and Blockchain in Finance

Shaping the Future of Finance

AI and blockchain are rapidly evolving, and their applications in finance are expanding. Emerging technologies, such as quantum computing, decentralized finance (DeFi), and advanced AI models, are poised to push the boundaries of what's possible in the financial sector. In this chapter, we'll explore the future trends that are likely to shape AI and blockchain's role in finance, driving innovation and creating new opportunities for efficiency, security, and transparency.

1. Quantum Computing and Its Impact on Blockchain and AI

Quantum computing, which operates on the principles of quantum mechanics, has the potential to solve complex problems much faster than classical computers. This technology holds immense promise for finance, particularly in areas like risk analysis, optimization, and cryptography.

Quantum's Impact on Blockchain Security

Blockchain relies heavily on cryptographic security, but quantum computers could theoretically break many of the cryptographic algorithms currently used. This poses both a threat and an opportunity for blockchain security, as finance institutions explore quantum-resistant cryptographic methods.

- **Example**: Financial institutions and blockchain

developers are beginning to research quantum-safe cryptography to protect blockchains from potential threats posed by quantum computers. Developing these algorithms will be essential for future-proofing blockchain's security.

Quantum's Potential for AI and Financial Modeling

Quantum computing could revolutionize AI by processing data and training models at unprecedented speeds, enabling financial institutions to perform complex calculations in areas like asset pricing, portfolio optimization, and market forecasting.

- **Example**: By using quantum-enhanced AI, banks could improve the accuracy of financial models, helping them assess risks with greater precision and make faster, data-driven decisions in volatile markets.

2. Decentralized Finance (DeFi): A New Era of Financial Services

DeFi, or decentralized finance, represents a significant shift away from traditional finance by enabling financial transactions without intermediaries like banks or brokers. Built on blockchain, DeFi uses smart contracts to offer services such as lending, borrowing, and trading in a peer-to-peer environment.

Benefits of DeFi in Finance

DeFi creates a more inclusive financial ecosystem by providing open access to financial services for anyone with an internet connection. Additionally, it reduces fees, increases transaction speeds, and eliminates the need for intermediaries.

- **Example**: Platforms like **AAVE** and **Compound** allow users to lend and borrow cryptocurrency assets directly, earning interest on deposits or obtaining loans without going through a bank. This model has the potential to reshape traditional banking services, making them more accessible and cost-effective.

DeFi Challenges and Regulatory Considerations

While DeFi offers many benefits, it also raises challenges around security and regulation. Since DeFi platforms are decentralized and rely on user-governed protocols, they lack the protections and oversight of traditional financial systems, posing risks for users.

- **Example**: Regulatory bodies worldwide are exploring frameworks to govern DeFi platforms to ensure they comply with financial standards and protect consumers from potential risks, such as cyber threats or market manipulation.

3. AI-Powered Predictive Analytics and Personalization

As AI models become more advanced, finance professionals can leverage predictive analytics to gain deeper insights into consumer behavior, market trends, and investment risks. Personalization in finance will also expand, allowing institutions to offer tailored financial advice and product recommendations.

Predictive Analytics in Investment and Risk Management

Predictive analytics enables financial institutions to assess risks and predict market movements more accurately. With AI models capable of processing vast amounts of data in real-time, finance teams can make more informed investment decisions and mitigate potential risks.

- **Example**: AI-driven predictive analytics models can analyze real-time data from global markets to forecast potential shifts, allowing hedge funds and investment firms to adjust their portfolios proactively.

Hyper-Personalization in Financial Services

AI is advancing personalization in finance by analyzing individual customer data to provide customized services. This trend is creating more personalized interactions, from investment recommendations to tailored insurance plans, which enhance customer satisfaction and loyalty.

- **Example**: Wealth management firms use AI to analyze a client's financial goals, spending habits, and risk tolerance to recommend personalized investment portfolios. Platforms like **Betterment** and **Wealthfront** leverage AI to automate this process, providing high-quality advisory services at scale.

4. Blockchain and Tokenization of Assets

Tokenization is the process of converting real-world assets, such as real estate, stocks, or commodities, into digital tokens on the blockchain. Tokenization enables fractional ownership, greater liquidity, and more efficient asset transfers, making it easier to trade traditionally illiquid assets.

Applications of Tokenization in Finance

Tokenization opens new investment opportunities for retail and institutional investors, allowing them to purchase fractional ownership of high-value assets. This democratizes access to assets that were once available only to wealthy investors, such as real estate or fine art.

- **Example**: **Tokeny** is a platform that allows businesses to tokenize assets like real estate or corporate bonds, enabling investors to buy shares in these assets via blockchain. This enhances liquidity and simplifies the investment process for traditionally illiquid markets.

Regulatory Implications of Tokenized Assets

Tokenized assets require a regulatory framework that addresses ownership rights, custody, and compliance. As more financial institutions adopt tokenization, regulators are likely to introduce guidelines to govern these digital assets and ensure they meet industry standards.

- **Example**: Regulatory agencies like the U.S. Securities

and Exchange Commission (SEC) are beginning to address digital assets to clarify their status as securities and outline guidelines for their legal use in investment portfolios.

5. Privacy-Enhancing Technologies (PETs) in Blockchain and AI

As privacy concerns grow, privacy-enhancing technologies (PETs) are gaining importance. PETs, such as zero-knowledge proofs (ZKPs) and homomorphic encryption, allow financial institutions to protect sensitive information without compromising data transparency or usability.

Zero-Knowledge Proofs for Data Privacy

ZKPs allow one party to prove to another that a statement is true without revealing any additional information. In finance, ZKPs enable institutions to verify transactions without exposing the underlying data, protecting customer privacy.

- **Example**: **Zcash**, a privacy-focused cryptocurrency, uses zero-knowledge proofs to ensure transaction confidentiality on its blockchain. Financial institutions could adopt similar approaches to protect client data while maintaining transparency.

Homomorphic Encryption for Secure Data Processing

Homomorphic encryption allows encrypted data to be processed without needing to decrypt it, enabling secure computations on sensitive information. This technology is particularly valuable for AI applications that require access to personal or financial data.

- **Example**: Banks could use homomorphic encryption to analyze customer spending habits for marketing insights without compromising the privacy of individual transactions. This allows them to use data-driven insights while ensuring data security.

6. Self-Regulating Smart Contracts

As smart contracts become more advanced, self-regulating smart contracts could allow for automated adjustments based on updated compliance requirements or market conditions. This trend will increase contract flexibility and compliance automation.

- **Example**: A self-regulating smart contract could automatically adjust interest rates on a loan based on changes in market rates, or it could pause transactions if regulatory compliance thresholds are met. This adaptability would reduce manual intervention and improve compliance in real time.

The Future Landscape of Finance: A Technology-Driven Ecosystem

These trends illustrate a future finance sector that is highly automated, transparent, and secure. AI and blockchain will continue to complement each other, with AI enabling predictive insights and blockchain providing secure, decentralized infrastructure. As privacy-enhancing technologies and quantum computing evolve, the finance industry will gain more tools to protect data while delivering innovative financial services.

Chapter Summary

The future of finance is one of transformation, driven by advances in AI, blockchain, and emerging technologies. Quantum computing, DeFi, predictive analytics, tokenization, and privacy-enhancing technologies will redefine finance, making it more inclusive, transparent, and efficient. Finance professionals who embrace these trends and develop the necessary skills will be well-positioned to lead in this new era of technology-driven finance.

CHAPTER 10

Conclusion and Practical Takeaways

Embracing the Future of Finance with AI and Blockchain

As we've explored throughout this book, AI and blockchain are fundamentally transforming the finance industry. From automating routine tasks and enhancing data security to revolutionizing auditing and creating a decentralized financial ecosystem, these technologies are reshaping what's possible in finance. However, with new technologies come new challenges, including ethical considerations, regulatory hurdles, and implementation obstacles.

For finance professionals and institutions, the path forward involves not only adopting these technologies but also developing the skills and strategies to navigate their complexities. As AI and blockchain continue to evolve, staying informed and agile will be key to leveraging their full potential.

Key Takeaways for Finance Professionals

1. Invest in Continuous Learning

As AI, blockchain, and other emerging technologies develop, continuous learning will be essential for finance professionals. Staying updated on the latest trends, gaining hands-on experience with digital tools, and obtaining certifications in AI, blockchain, or data analytics can enhance your skillset and prepare you for new roles in finance.

- **Action Step**: Consider enrolling in online courses or attending workshops on AI, blockchain, and data science to build expertise and stay competitive in the industry.

2. Adopt a Data-Driven Mindset

AI and blockchain are fueled by data, and finance professionals must develop a data-driven approach to make effective decisions. By understanding how to interpret data analytics, assess risks, and spot patterns, you can make more informed financial decisions and contribute valuable insights to your organization.

- **Action Step**: Practice working with data analytics tools like Tableau, Power BI, or Excel to analyze data trends and make data-driven recommendations.

3. Understand the Ethical and Regulatory Implications

The ethical and regulatory landscape for AI and blockchain is complex and constantly evolving. Finance professionals need to be aware of issues like data privacy, algorithmic bias, and compliance to ensure that they use these technologies responsibly and in alignment with industry standards.

- **Action Step**: Stay informed about regulatory changes by following updates from financial regulatory bodies, joining industry groups, or participating in ethics seminars focused on AI and blockchain.

4. Collaborate Across Disciplines

As AI and blockchain adoption grows, finance professionals will need to collaborate closely with data scientists, IT specialists, and compliance officers. Building interdisciplinary knowledge and working with cross-functional teams will improve the integration of these technologies into your organization's financial operations.

- **Action Step**: Engage with colleagues in data science

or IT departments to deepen your understanding of technical challenges and collaborate on implementing solutions.

5. Embrace Innovation with an Open Mind

The finance industry is rapidly changing, and those who are willing to experiment and innovate will be at the forefront of this transformation. Embrace new tools, pilot new processes, and be open to the possibilities that AI and blockchain offer for streamlining operations and enhancing security.

- **Action Step**: Seek out opportunities within your organization to pilot AI or blockchain projects, even on a small scale, to gain practical experience and explore the technology's potential.

Practical Steps for Finance Organizations

1. Start with Small-Scale Implementations

For organizations just beginning to explore AI and blockchain, starting with small pilot projects can be an effective way to test their value. For example, implementing RPA in a single department or piloting blockchain for a specific auditing process allows you to evaluate the technology's impact before making large investments.

2. Develop a Governance Framework

As AI and blockchain adoption grows, it's essential to have a governance framework that addresses ethical standards, data privacy, and compliance requirements. This framework should outline best practices for responsible AI and blockchain usage, establish accountability, and guide decision-making.

3. Invest in Skills Development for Employees

As these technologies reshape finance roles, organizations should prioritize skills development for their employees. Training programs, certifications, and hands-on workshops can help employees build the technical and analytical skills they need to succeed in a digital finance environment.

4. Collaborate with Regulatory Bodies

To ensure compliance and stay ahead of regulatory changes, finance organizations should engage proactively with regulatory bodies. This collaboration can provide insights into upcoming regulations and help institutions align their technology implementations with industry standards.

The Road Ahead

The journey toward a technology-driven finance sector is just beginning. With AI and blockchain, finance professionals have tools that enable them to focus on high-value, strategic tasks while improving accuracy, efficiency, and security. The future of finance will likely be marked by further integration of these technologies, along with the emergence of new innovations such as quantum computing, DeFi, and privacy-enhancing technologies.

As we move forward, those who embrace the transformative power of AI and blockchain, while addressing their ethical and regulatory implications, will be well-positioned to thrive in the evolving landscape. Finance professionals and organizations that take proactive steps to adopt, adapt, and innovate will play a leading role in shaping the future of finance.

Final Thoughts

AI and blockchain represent a new era for finance—a future where technology enables smarter, faster, and more secure financial practices. By leveraging the knowledge, skills, and tools discussed in this book, finance professionals can confidently navigate this transformation and lead the way in creating a financial sector that is inclusive, resilient, and responsive to the needs of tomorrow.

Thank you for embarking on this journey through AI and blockchain in finance. May this knowledge empower you to innovate, adapt, and contribute to a future where finance and technology go hand in hand.

Bibliography/References

Books

1. Agrawal, A., Gans, J., & Goldfarb, A. (2018). *Prediction Machines: The Simple Economics of Artificial Intelligence.* Harvard Business Review Press.
   - A comprehensive introduction to the impact of AI on decision-making and its applications across industries, including finance.

2. Tapscott, D., & Tapscott, A. (2016). *Blockchain Revolution: How the Technology Behind Bitcoin and Other Cryptocurrencies is Changing the World.* Portfolio.
   - An insightful look into blockchain technology and its potential to revolutionize finance and other industries.

3. Marr, B. (2020). *Artificial Intelligence in Practice: How 50 Successful Companies Used AI and Machine Learning to Solve Problems.* Wiley.
   - This book covers real-world applications of AI across different sectors, including finance, providing practical examples for beginners and professionals.

4. Narayanan, A., Bonneau, J., Felten, E., Miller, A., & Goldfeder, S. (2016). *Bitcoin and Cryptocurrency Technologies.* Princeton University Press.
   - A thorough technical exploration of blockchain and cryptocurrencies, ideal for readers interested in understanding blockchain technology in depth.

Articles and Research Papers

1. Verma, S., & Rahman, M. H. (2019). "Applications of Artificial Intelligence in Financial Markets."

International Journal of Financial Studies, 7(3), 36.
   - This paper discusses various AI applications in finance, covering predictive analytics, fraud detection, and algorithmic trading.

2. Zheng, Z., Xie, S., Dai, H., Chen, X., & Wang, H. (2017). "An Overview of Blockchain Technology: Architecture, Consensus, and Future Trends." *2017 IEEE International Congress on Big Data.*
   - A useful resource on blockchain's technical framework, consensus mechanisms, and potential applications.

3. Kharif, O. (2018). "How AI Is Transforming Finance." *Bloomberg.*
   - An accessible overview of how AI is being implemented in finance, with examples and perspectives from industry leaders.

Reports and White Papers

1. Deloitte. (2020). *AI in Financial Services: How Artificial Intelligence is Transforming Financial Institutions.*
   - A report on AI adoption in financial services, exploring current uses, benefits, and challenges faced by institutions.

2. IBM. (2019). *Blockchain for Financial Services: Building Trust in a Digital Economy.*
   - This report provides insights into blockchain's impact on finance, focusing on secure transactions, transparency, and the shift toward decentralized finance (DeFi).

3. McKinsey & Company. (2020). *The Future of Work in Financial Services.*
   - A report covering how AI and automation

are reshaping roles in financial services, with a focus on necessary skills and workforce transformation.

Web Resources

1. CoinDesk - www.coindesk.com
   - A leading source for blockchain news, covering cryptocurrency developments, DeFi, and blockchain's impact on finance.

2. MIT Technology Review - www.technologyreview.com
   - A resource for current research and articles on emerging technologies, including AI and blockchain, with insights into their implications for finance.

3. Harvard Business Review - www.hbr.org
   - A reputable resource featuring articles on digital transformation, AI in business, and the future of finance.

4. Investopedia - www.investopedia.com
   - Offers accessible articles on blockchain, cryptocurrency, and AI, providing definitions, explanations, and practical examples.

www.ingramcontent.com/pod-product-compliance
Lightning Source LLC
Chambersburg PA
CBHW030504220526
45464CB00006B/2649